# THE PITTED NAIL

## My Rescue, God's Grace

Kenneth Pullin

Published in the United States of America by

Spirit Media and our logos are trademarks of Spirit Media Inc
205 Academy Street #3251 – Cary, NC 27519
1 (888) 800-3744 | https://spiritmedia.us

Books | Christian Living | Inspirational
Books | Biography & Autobiography | Religious

THE PITTED NAIL

Paperback ISBN: 979-8-89307-223-5
eBook ISBN: 979-8-89307-214-3
PDF ISBN: 979-8-89307-215-0

Library of Congress Control Number: Applied

# Acknowledgements

I would like to extend my heartfelt thanks to John Johnson for contributing the concept and illustration for the front cover.

I am also deeply grateful to Lula Hopkins for providing the inspiring subtitle idea.

Your creativity and support have played a significant role in bringing this story to life.

We are proud supporters of Tunnel to Towers and the Wounded Warriors project. A donation will be made to both organizations in lieu of sales in honor of the important work they do.

# Dedication

This book is dedicated to all those who, like the Pitted Nail, have been through the storms of life that changed their appearance and re-shaped the original person you once were. Sometimes going through the tough times of life can cause a process called hormesis or (work hardening) effect. In other words, the tougher it gets the stronger you become.

The Pitted Nail was a perfect example of this in a true sense. The last thing we would have thought of using in the situation we were in was that weathered, bent, rusted and pitted old nail. But we didn't know it had a special purpose and that it was to rise to the occasion at hand. You see it was changed by erosion to be stronger than a new nail which held the future for two young men with new families and so much more we would do to impact the world we live in. Think of all the people who have been through events that changed their abilities to perform in a normal way. Now they must accomplish tasks in a whole new way. They too have been weatherbeaten and scared by the trials of life.

I especially want to dedicate this story to a very close friend that went through this storm with me. For only he and I will ever know what it was really like out there on that water during this event, and now I'm the only one left to tell it like it was. Rest in Peace my friend for your storms come no more.

# Contents

# Still Waters

*"$H$<small>E SAYS, 'B<small>E STILL</small>, and know that I am God;</small>*
*I will be exalted among the nations,*
*I will be exalted in the earth.'" — Psalm 46:10 (NIV)*

*Faith begins in stillness and everyday obedience.*

As I thumb through the pages of my life, memories flash like snapshots in my mind—moments that shaped who I became. When I was a young boy, and even into my twenties, I had more than my share of close calls with nature. I once stepped into an old, rotted-out pine tree stump that was home to a nasty hive of Yellow Jackets. On another occasion, I dove into a muddy river not knowing what lay beneath. God's fingerprints were on everything in my life, though I didn't see it then. I didn't yet understand His grace, but it had already taken hold of me. Looking back now, I can see how His mercy often stood between me and disaster. But one day's brush with danger would change everything.

My childhood was stable and full of happy moments and lots of laughter. I was blessed with Christian parents who believed faith and family came first—exceptional role models for my brothers and me. We attended a small church where people prayed for one another, sang old hymns, and applied the lessons of the messages to their lives. Sunday mornings began with a quick bowl of cereal while everyone rushed to get ready for church. This was quite challenging since we only had one bathroom. After church, we all gathered around the table to enjoy whatever meal mom had prepared for the day. Sunday lunches are some of the best memories I will always cherish.

Many of my childhood memories were of the times we spent with my dad's family; we were extremely close. My dad's brothers and sisters were spread across Virginia, the Carolinas, Tennessee, and Florida. My mom was also close to her family, and she adored her parents. However, we didn't spend nearly as much time with that side of our family over the years; nonetheless, the love we had for one another was strong.

Every year, my dad's family made it a priority to get everyone together for a reunion. My cousins were more like siblings, and we all looked forward to our time together. The reunions lasted for days! Our family was full of jokesters, each one trying to outdo the others. There was never a gathering without laughter echoing through the house.

My Mom kept our home welcoming and filled with love. She was the best cook I've ever known. Sunday dinners and holiday feasts could have graced the pages of a magazine—golden turkey, cheese grits, and her shoofly pies that never lasted long. My mom also had quite a sense of humor. One Sunday after church, my mom made it inside the house before the rest of us. She then peered out the door and, in a startled voice, announced she had forgotten to turn on the stove, and we had no meal. My younger brother squealed in disappointment at the news, but of course, my mom was joking. We all laughed. Her laughter filled the house as surely as the smell of her cooking. Even her teasing carried warmth.

Money was tight, but we never felt poor. "Hand-me-downs" were just another way of sharing blessings. I even wore the same shirt in my school pictures two years in a row. Dad worked for Bell-Atlantic by day and fixed wrecked cars in our garage by night—buying damaged company cars, rebuilding them, and selling them for a little extra money. He would come home by six, eat supper with us, and then disappear into the glow of that single drop-light until well into the night. I often held the light for him, trying not to shake the light while he was working. If you've ever been asked to do this job, you know the importance of a steady hand. No one worked harder than my dad. I recently overheard my son make that same comment about me, and I realized in that moment how much my dad had shaped my life.

*Faith ain't just believing. It's doing.*

I learned that first from watching my parents, long before I understood it myself. My dad often said, "More is caught than taught," and that is undoubtedly true. They didn't talk much about faith; they just lived it, committed and faithful, every day that God gave them.

We didn't have many toys, but we had the outdoors. Ants, chipmunks, bees, and the creek beside our home were our playground. The woods stretched like a secret world waiting to be discovered. The woods were my first adventure; the water became my second.

My older brother's friends often came by to play football. They were older and many of them had a different upbringing than we did, so many games ended in unsportsmanlike conduct. Fishing always sounded like a better pastime for me. Around the age of eleven, I got my first Zebco 33 reel and a pocketknife, which I still keep in my tackle box to this day. That was the beginning of my lifelong love for fishing. I'd sit for hours, just waiting for that line to twitch. The sun would sink low before I'd give up for the day. Patience came slowly, but when it did, it stuck. I reckon that's where I first learned how quiet could feel like company. I didn't know it then, but God was already teaching me how to listen.

My dad never cared much for fishing—he didn't even like to eat fish—so I taught myself. There was something about patience and silence that felt like its own kind of church. I practiced casting in the yard, tying a nut to my line, and aiming for fence posts until I could hit any spot I wanted. Sometimes, the nut would get caught on a root or rock when I was reeling it back in. I would pretend I was navigating a large bass through the water until it broke free.

Our house was situated near a lake that supplied the local swimming area. I'd hike up the hill past the creek until I reached the dam. The path led through old Civil War campsites, where bits of tin and bullets still surfaced in the dirt. There, the lily pads grew thick and green, the water dark and alive; the crappy and bass were plentiful in that spot. That place was a haven to me—I can still smell the mix of moss, mud, and pine. A little farther around the curve of the lake, just beyond an old barbed wire fence, a holly tree had fallen across the water. The branches remained green years after the tree fell. I'd cast beneath those limbs, and the fish were always waiting.

When you sit still long enough, you start to hear things you'd been too busy to notice before—the hum of the line, the splash of a turtle, the whisper of your own thoughts. Those summers taught me patience and a kind of faith you don't learn in church. There was peace in the waiting and a quiet joy in knowing that the One who made the water was watching over me. Those moments on the lake stayed with me long after I packed up my tackle box for the last time.

As years passed, the woods turned into neighborhoods. I traded those long afternoons by the lake for a full-time job and grown-up responsibilities. At twenty-five, I built my first home and left the shelter of my parents' roof. I worked hard, chasing the security every young man wants. I held many jobs from warehouse work to electrical wiring to sales, and eventually found that talking with people came as naturally as breathing. But easy seasons can dull a man's hearing, and I didn't notice how quiet God had gone in my life until that summer came. I married, became a father, and thought I had life figured out. But beneath all that busyness, a restlessness stirred. Something was missing.

My distance from God would become glaringly evident one summer morning on the Chesapeake Bay, when my faith, and my life, would be tested in ways I never expected. The stillness of those lakeside days had taught me how to wait, but not how to listen. It would take another body of water, and a storm far greater than any I'd faced, to bring that lesson home.

# Into the Fog

"*T*RUST IN THE LORD *with all your heart and lean not on your own understanding.*" — *Proverbs 3:5 (NIV)*

*Warnings ignored lead to lessons remembered.*
*(George Santayana)*

In the summer of 1989, at twenty-eight years old, my good friend Joe and I planned a trip to go fishing on a Saturday in the Chesapeake Bay. It had been one of those long workweeks that left me hungry for the outdoors, and when Joe called, it didn't take much convincing. I needed the water, the quiet, and that kind of friendship where you don't have to talk much to feel understood.

We borrowed his dad's fourteen-foot Boston Whaler, a boat so famously tough that people said you could saw it in half and it would still float. Joe was proud of that little boat and said it could handle anything the Bay threw at us. Still, that was a theory I didn't want to test.

We were old enough to know better, but not by much. That kind of confidence has a way of whispering, "What could go wrong?" right before it does.

Joe's dad had warned us that the shear pin had been breaking lately and told us not to go too far. I nodded, but I already knew we'd be tempted to push it. That's how we were wired. Two grown men chasing the same kind of adventure that used to get us in trouble as boys. I laughed it off at the time, but his words sat in the back of my mind like a splinter, "Boy, a warning ignored is a lesson repeated." His voice still followed me like a conscience I hadn't quite outgrown. We should have listened more closely. *The fear of the Lord is the beginning of knowledge, but fools despise wisdom and instruction (Proverbs 1:7; KJV).* That verse had followed me since my early days of Sunday school. Somewhere between paychecks, diapers, and bills, I'd let the noise of life drown it out. But even then, God's Word had a way of circling back when I needed it most.

The forecast promised fog in the morning and a slight chance of storms later in the day.

Joe brushed it off, but I've never completely trusted that phrase, *slight chance of storms.* Those are the ones that sneak up on you. Still, the thought of open water was too tempting. I told myself we'd play it smart and head in early if the weather turned.

That's the trouble with "slight chances." They always sound harmless until you're the fool standing in the middle of one.

The night before, I lay awake staring at the ceiling, restless with anticipation. One thing that weighed on me was the fact that I get motion sickness, so the thought of possible rough waters caused a little anxiety. I finally drifted off sometime after midnight in the complete silence of the room. The next thing I remember was a tug on my shoulder. Joe was saying it was time to head out to the dock. It felt too early for two men who had stayed up late the evening before, but we were both excited to start the day.

We didn't talk much as we got ready to leave. Trying to be as quiet as possible, we eased the back door shut so as not to wake Joe's dad. The moment we stepped outside, the fog hit us in the face like a wall of wet cotton—soundless, heavy, and close enough to taste. I'd never seen it quite so thick before.

The fog hugged the trees on either side of the path, soft and gray, the kind of quiet that makes you think of prayer even when you haven't said one in a while. As we made our way down the steep path to the dock, every step felt uncertain. The air was thick, and I could barely see Joe's outline a few steps ahead.

We'd been in tight spots before. One spring, we were turkey hunting when a cold front hit without warning. The temperature dropped rapidly in a matter of minutes, the wind whipping through the trees all around us. Tree limbs were snapping and bending everywhere, and the wind was so loud we couldn't hear our calls to each other. Suddenly, Joe appeared on the hill through the woods. With the light shining behind him, it reminded me of a war movie, where a soldier stands on the crest of a battlefield appearing as a dark silhouette. But this fog felt different—too quiet, too close, like the Bay itself was holding its breath.

We finally reached the dock and climbed into the boat. We untied, pushed off, and eased forward into the gray. The fog swallowed the shoreline until there was nothing left but the low hum of the motor and the sound of our own breathing. I told myself it was just another day on the water, but somewhere deep down, I knew this trip would be different from the others.

We crept forward, barely above an idle, cautious of what we couldn't see. The creek was narrow, thirty yards at most, and the fog so thick we couldn't tell where the water ended and the land began. Every few seconds, Joe eased off the throttle so we wouldn't hit anything. My nerves buzzed with every hum of the motor. It was like floating inside a Styrofoam cup—white all around, hollow, and fragile.

My stomach gave a slow, uneasy roll. I've never handled motion well. When I was a kid, Mom had a home remedy she swore by. If I got carsick, she'd cut a square from a brown grocery bag and place it right on my stomach, saying it would help draw out the nausea. I don't know how, but it always seemed to work. I smiled at the memory, then frowned, wishing I'd brought one along. The damp air already felt like it was stirring something queasy deep inside me. There is a funny thing about old remedies: they work best when you believe they will. I reckon that was faith of a different kind.

By the time we reached the small marina, the fog seemed even thicker over the water.

The seagulls were already awake and fussing over scraps near the pilings. There was a faint smell of exhaust mixed with salt air and mud. If there's a scent that says coastal Virginia, that was it. The docks creaked under our boots like old floorboards that had heard every story. The ropes groaned, the hulls nudged the piers with a slow *thunk-thunk,* and somewhere a bell clanged faint and hollow in the fog. My boots slipped on the wet planks, and for the first time that morning, I felt a tightness in my gut. Feeling a bit anxious, I tried to laugh it off, but my stomach wasn't cooperating.

An older man in overalls stood at the end of the dock, coiling rope with slow, aged hands. He said something about it not being a good morning to be boating and that the Bay had her moods. Joe smiled and gave a small wave, but I didn't say anything; it was still too early for conversations. There was something in that man's tone, part warning and part wisdom, that settled deep in my chest. It wasn't just his words; it was the way he said them—slow, like he'd seen men disappear into that same fog and never come back the same. Joe didn't seem concerned in the slightest, but I was feeling a tinge of apprehension about the day.

As I walked down that old dock, I noticed a sixteen-penny galvanized nail, shaped like an L. It was old, pitted, and weather-beaten. It looked like it had already seen all the life it was going to see. My dad would've kept a nail like that; he found a use for everything. I kicked it with the toe of my shoe, meaning to knock it off the dock into the water. Instead, it bounced down the boards, clinking every few feet for about sixteen feet of that twenty-foot dock, until the last bounce sent it skipping off the edge of the boat and straight into the drain-well at the back. Joe went into the shop at the marina to purchase some shear pins for the boat in case we had issues. There were no shear pins available, so Joe bought a handful (eight) of sixteen-penny nails instead. He figured they would be a good substitute for the shear pin if the need arose.

# Through the Storm

"HE STILLED THE STORM to a whisper;
the waves of the sea were hushed." — Psalm 107:29 (NIV)

*God's grace holds when nothing else does.*

Once aboard, the fog was beginning to lift and visibility was improving. The sun was starting to burn off the fog, and I was feeling more optimistic about the day. The water was calm and beautiful, and the weather was perfect in that moment. Joe engaged the throttle, and we planned the water perfectly as we headed out into the bay.

We passed the last marker post and eased into open water. The still air carried only the sound of the motor and the faint slosh of the water behind us. I remember thinking how wide the Bay looked that morning—the shoreline fading from sight, only pale water and sky melting together. It was beautiful in a quiet, uneasy way.

Our course was to shoot straight out of the mouth of the creek and directly into the middle of the Chesapeake Bay. We headed out for about fifteen miles before we stopped to fish. There was no shoreline in sight in one direction and barely a sign of a tree line in the other direction. We decided we were far enough out, and Joe cut the engine. We sat in that spot for hours, fishing, or so we thought. The tide was going out, so our boat was moving further into the bay than we realized. Nonetheless, we had a great time talking about our younger years and enjoying the peacefulness of the day.

I remember thinking how days like this had always felt like a kind of promise to me. Something about the water, smooth as glass, made me feel closer to God even when I wasn't living like it. Out there on the water, everything else faded away for a while.

Mid-afternoon, we noticed some dark clouds in the distance. The rapid change in the air happened first. It had that sharp, metallic smell that always comes before a storm, like the Bay itself drawing a deep breath. The gulls that had been circling a few minutes before were gone. The line of dark clouds that stretched low on the horizon started creeping toward us faster than seemed possible. I told myself it would slip right past us, but in minutes the air turned cooler and the water rougher, the surface rippling like wrinkled tin.

The rain started as a mist, then came sideways. The wind carried it in hard bursts that stung our faces. Waves began to slap the sides of the Whaler—short and sharp at first, then taller, heavier. Joe started the engine as we both prepared for a bumpy ride back. The storm was no longer coming, it was on top of us.

The Bay, calm a moment before, now looked alive and angry. Water heaved in gray folds; gusts tore at our jackets. As Joe engaged the throttle, we heard a loud ZING! We knew that sound; the shear pin snapped. When the engine died, the silence that followed was even more profound than the wind had been. We looked at one another without speaking, and I felt a terrible wave of anxiety come over me.

Replacing a shear pin wasn't an easy task in calm waters, and the waters around us were anything but calm. We faced another challenge: the motor lock that held the engine in place for Joe to change the shear pin was broken, so this one-person job required both of us to work together. Joe tilted the motor out of the water and lay across it. I held the motor down so it didn't fall forward and launch Joe into the water. Joe pulled the cotter pin, unscrewed the nut, slid off the prop, broke a sixteen-penny nail to length, and fed it through while the boat pitched and rolled. Joe would hand each piece to me to hold throughout the process. The wind climbed; lightning flashed in the distance. The waves tossing the boat back and forth made this process much more challenging. He reattached the prop, tightened everything down, and started the engine. As soon as he engaged the throttle, we heard that dreadful sound again-ZING!

The boat began to drift, rocking harder as the waves built. Each rise lifted us high enough to see whitecaps all around, then dropped us into a trough where the horizon vanished.

The Bay had turned mean. The wind roared across the water, whipping the surface into whitecaps that slapped against the hull like open hands. Each wave tossed us higher, and the boat slammed down harder into the water.

One nail after another gave way. It seemed like each nail broke faster than the one before. Every sound made my stomach tighten. I wasn't feeling anxiety anymore; I was experiencing fear like I had never known. There were no cell phones, we didn't have a flare, and there were no other boats in sight.

The process was complicated, and we were growing weak from all the work. As Joe lay across the engine for the eighth and last time, I said a silent prayer. I found myself making deals with God, saying that if He would bring us through this, I would live differently. Joe completed the process and reattached the prop. He started the engine and engaged the throttle. The engine grabbed, and we began to move forward. We both breathed a deep sigh of relief. We still had to ride through this storm, but at least we had a chance. Then we heard that terrible sound one last time- ZING!

That was it. We were out of nails and out of options. Panic started to set in. I got lost in my thoughts for a moment, thinking of my baby girl back at home. What would her life be like growing up without her dad? She didn't really know me yet, but I knew her. I thought about my parents and my friends. Was it really going to end like this? For a moment, I thought we could ride out the storm, but then the rain on my face brought me back to the harsh reality of the situation.

By then, the Bay was a battlefield. Three- and four-foot seas lifted and dropped us like a toy. Rain pelted sideways; thunder cracked close enough to rattle the motor mount. I fought against my thoughts, but they were flooding my mind. What was it going to be like to drown? I knew there was no way we could survive if the waves overtook our boat. The fear on Joe's face made the situation even worse.

I was praying between all the thoughts. Part of me felt I had no right to pray because I had not been living my life the way I should, but part of me believed God still cared for me.

Suddenly, I remembered the old pitted nail I'd kicked off the dock that morning—the one that wasn't supposed to be there. I almost didn't even mention it to Joe because I thought there was no way that beat-up old nail could do what all the new nails couldn't do. Still, I had to tell him if there was a chance at all.

I bailed water from the drain well and saw it. That same pitted nail I had seen no use for that morning. It was wedged in the hole, battered and rust-streaked, but it was there. That nail, the one that shouldn't have been on board, was now our lifeline. *The stone the builders rejected has become the cornerstone - Psalm 118:22 (NIV)*

We were both on the verge of accepting our fate. My arms were shaking from holding the motor, and Joe was exhausted, but we mustered the strength to go through the process one more time. Joe set that pitted nail in place and pushed the starter. I was praying. The motor caught. As Joe eased the throttle— *ka-chugg!* —The boat lunged forward. The nail held. Neither of us breathed for the first few seconds. I yelled, "Don't touch that throttle!" and he didn't. We stayed at a crawl, the bow slapping every wave like a heartbeat.

Lightning split the sky. The rain blurred the horizon from the sea, and every flash revealed a wall of gray around us. Hymns drifted through my mind, *Till the Storm Passes By* and *Rock of Ages*, not sung aloud, just felt like prayers stitched into the noise. Then, topping one wave, I saw the tree line again, tiny and no taller than my thumb. Land.

How much longer could that nail hold? Why was something so bent and used up stronger than all the new ones? Maybe because God still had a purpose for it. That thought steadied me.

The boat slammed down again— *bam!* —spray flying over us. Water poured into the bottom faster than we could bail. The weight made it harder on the prop, and the nail groaned against the strain. The lightning cracked so close it was like shotgun fire beside our ears. I found myself whispering, "Lord, please let it last another mile."

Another issue to add to the list: gas. We didn't have a built-in tank, just a single can, and with the motor running slow, we were burning more than usual. I lifted it. There was ten, maybe fifteen percent left. *Will this be enough to make it back?*

Didn't matter much what I thought, though. God already knew.

Joe stayed quiet. The storm drifted north, following the Bay while we turned west toward the Rappahannock River. What a sight: home water, close enough to stir hope. Still, the channel was shallow in places, and if the prop struck bottom, that nail would shear for sure.

Where the Chesapeake meets the Atlantic, the great rivers empty one by one: the James, the York, the Piankatank, and then the Rappahannock, our stop. I thanked God Joe knew every curve and creek, because I'd never have found my way back alone.

As we entered the creek where the day had begun, emotions hit harder than the wind ever had: relief, disbelief, gratitude, all mixed together. Only someone who's fought water like that could understand the fear, the help-lessness, the miracle of simply making it back.

That bent, weather-beaten nail—just a piece of metal—had carried two young men fifteen miles through a treacherous storm by the grace of God. When I think of these events, a song comes to mind: *The Anchor Holds.* As I look back now, I see how the hand of God was upon my life that day and has been throughout my life.

I often think of Jesus and those three nails that held Jesus to the cross. If anyone ever knew the power of a nail, it was Him. The world rejected Him, too. Still, He held fast so we could live.

Some folks think they're no good, that life's storms have left them too damaged, and they don't matter. But the pitted nail was bent, cut in half by rust and wear, and still, in God's hands, it did its job. Be that nail. Be the one who holds when everything else fails.

There wasn't anything else I could do. The rest was up to God.

# Back to Shore

"He said to his disciples, 'Why are you so afraid? Do you still have no faith?'" — Mark 4:40 (NIV)

*Peace doesn't mean calm seas—it means trusting who calms them.*

When we finally reached the dock, the sky was clearing. The rain had slowed to a drizzle, and the fog that had swallowed the Bay all morning now drifted apart in thin streaks. The air smelled of wet rope, exhaust, and wood that had soaked and dried a hundred times before. I don't remember climbing out of the boat, only the feeling of solid boards under my boots again. I knelt right there on the dock, water dripping from my sleeves, and thanked God we were home.

Joe's dad came down the hill with a towel over his shoulder, shaking his head. He didn't have to say a word. That look said it all: *You boys are lucky to be alive.* He helped tie off the boat, then stood back and just stared at the sky.

The storm had left its fingerprints everywhere. The surface of the Bay shimmered with broken light; bits of debris floated near the pilings—twigs, weeds, a plastic bottle turning in slow circles. The air felt lighter.

Joe didn't speak for a while. He just sat on the edge of the dock, head down, elbows on his knees, staring at the water. I joined him, both of us quiet. Words seemed too small for what we'd just come through. We were exhausted, humbled, and still a little stunned. Every sound—the gulls, the creak of the ropes, the slow slap of waves—felt magnified, holy somehow.

After a long while, he finally said, "That nail's going in a frame."

We both laughed, the kind of laugh that breaks tension and turns into something close to tears. I told him it belonged in his dad's workshop, right next to the hammer that probably drove it in thirty years ago. He grinned, shook his head, and said, "No. That one stays with the boat."

We removed the nail from the prop. I turned it over in my hand and thought about how something so ordinary could carry the weight of a miracle. It wasn't pretty, but it had done what it was made to do.

Driving home that afternoon, the world looked different. The same roads, the same trees, the same smell of pine and salt in the air, yet I saw it all with fresh eyes. The sun broke through the thinning clouds, washing the fields in gold. Everything seemed sharper, cleaner, alive.

I thought about the verse: *He stilled the storm to a whisper; the waves of the sea were hushed - Psalm 107:29 (NIV)*

I realized the storm wasn't the punishment. It was the rescue. It had stripped away everything I thought I could control, leaving only what mattered. God hadn't abandoned us out there; He'd met us in the middle of it.

By God's grace, I made it home to my little girl that day. I stood in the doorway and watched her crawl across the floor. I held her in my arms that night and thanked the

Lord for bringing me home to her. The steady rhythm of her breathing and the warmth of that small house felt like the purest blessing I'd ever known.

I have since been blessed to raise three children of my own and three children through marriage. Today, I am a proud Pop to twelve of the most beautiful grandchildren, and I just know God isn't finished with me yet!

Sometimes I still think about that day, the fog, the waves, and the nail that held. Life since then hasn't been free of storms, but I learned something no sermon could have taught me: grace isn't fragile, and God's hands don't slip.

We all have our storms. We all have our nails. The trick is remembering Who holds them.

The End.

# MORE FROM
# KENNETH W. PULLIN

# MORE FROM
# KENNETH W. PULLIN

# About the Author

Kenneth Pullin, a lifelong resident of Mechanicsville, Virginia, is an Account Manager, devoted husband to Trish, and proud father of six and grandfather of twelve. Kenneth brings the same dedication to his writing as he does to his career and family. Inspired by his personal walk with God, he writes to share the grace and goodness of the Lord through heartfelt stories. The author of two beloved children's books, Kenneth continues creating faith-filled works that inspire families to grow together in love, joy, and faith.